Letterland

Fix-it Phonics

My name is

Let's learn about...

s a t p i n m d

g o c k e u r

Level 1 - Workbook 1

Focus on sound

Find the objects starting with Sammy Snake's sound.
Then colour the picture.

sun   **s**ea   **s**and

Focus on sound

Draw lines from Sammy Snake to the things that start with his sound. Circle the one that doesn't.

Draw something that starts with Sammy Snake's sound.

Stick Sammy Snake's letter shape here.

Focus on shape

Let's write Sammy Snake's letter shape.

Let's write both his letter shapes.

Sammy Snake

Focus on sound

Find the objects starting with Annie Apple's sound.
Then colour the picture.

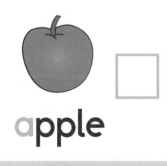

apple

arrow

ant

Focus on sound

Draw lines from Annie Apple to the things that start with her sound. Circle the one that doesn't.

Draw something that starts with Annie Apple's sound.

Stick Annie Apple's letter shape here.

Let's write Annie Apple's letter shape.

Let's write both her letter shapes.

Annie Apple

Focus on sound

Find the objects starting with Talking Tess's sound.
Then colour the picture.

table **toys** **10**
ten

Focus on sound

Draw lines from Talking Tess to the things that start with her sound. Circle the one that doesn't.

Draw something that starts with Talking Tess's sound.

Stick Talking Tess's letter shape here.

Let's write Talking Tess's letter shape.

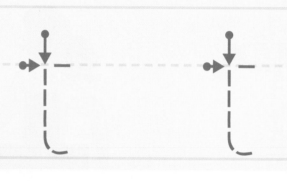

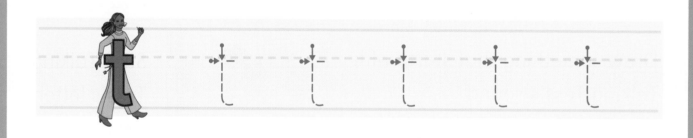

Let's write both her letter shapes.

Talking Tess

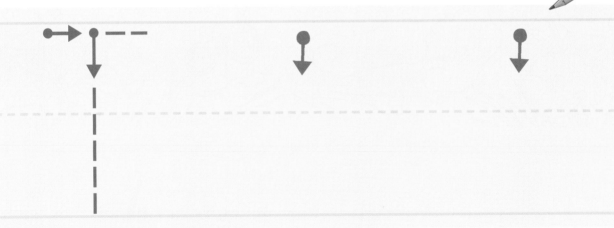

Focus on sound

Find the objects starting with Peter Puppy's sound.
Then colour the picture.

pen ☐

pencil ☐

paint ☐

Draw lines from Peter Puppy to the things that start with his sound. Circle the one that doesn't.

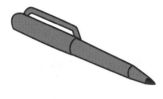

Draw something that starts with Peter Puppy's sound.

Stick Peter Puppy's letter shape here.

Focus on shape

Let's write Peter Puppy's letter shape.

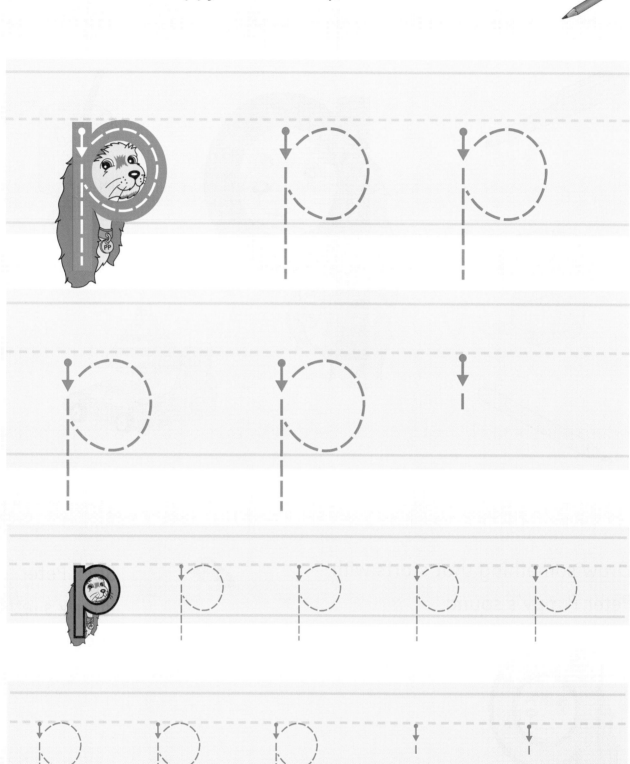

Let's write both his letter shapes.

Peter Puppy

Fill in the correct letters to make the words below.

s   a   t   p

_en   **10**

_un

_en

_nt

Phonic Word Builder

 Now write this word. Your Letterland friends are helping you below.

19

Put the correct Letterland stickers over the plain letter shapes.
Then draw lines to match them to their objects.

s

a

t

p

Letter sound Recognising the letter sound at the start of words is an important first step in language and literacy.

Listen

 Listen to the words and put a tick next to the one you hear. The first one has been done for you.

 CD 1 Track 18

1.  ✓   ☐   ☐

2.  ☐    ☐   ☐

3.  ☐   ☐    ☐

4.  ☐    ☐    ☐

5.  ☐    ☐    ☐

6. ☐   10 ☐   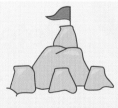 ☐

Can you find these characters hidden in the sentences below?
The first words have been done for you.

Sammy swims in the sea.

Sammy sits in the sun.

Can you see an ant?

The ant is on Annie Apple.

Talking Tess likes triangles.

Tess can play tennis.

Peter packs a picnic.

Peter plays in the park.

Focus on sound

Find the objects starting with Impy Ink's sound.
Then colour the picture.

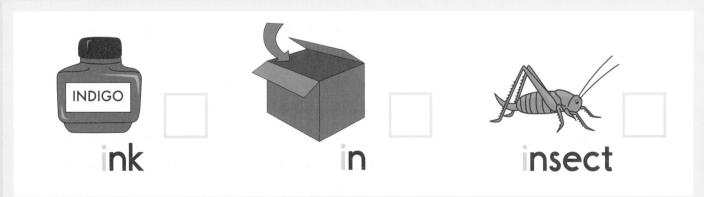

ink   in   insect

Focus on sound

Draw lines from Impy Ink to the things that start with his sound. Circle the one that doesn't.

INDIGO

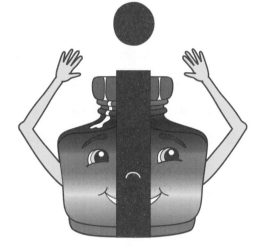

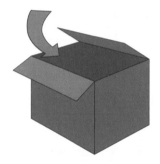

Draw something that starts with Impy Ink's sound.

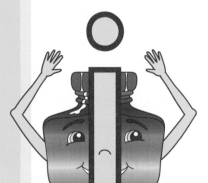

Stick Impy Ink's letter shape here.

Let's write Impy Ink's letter shape.

Let's write both his letter shapes.

Impy   Ink

Focus on sound

Find the objects starting with Noisy Nick's sound.
Then colour the picture.

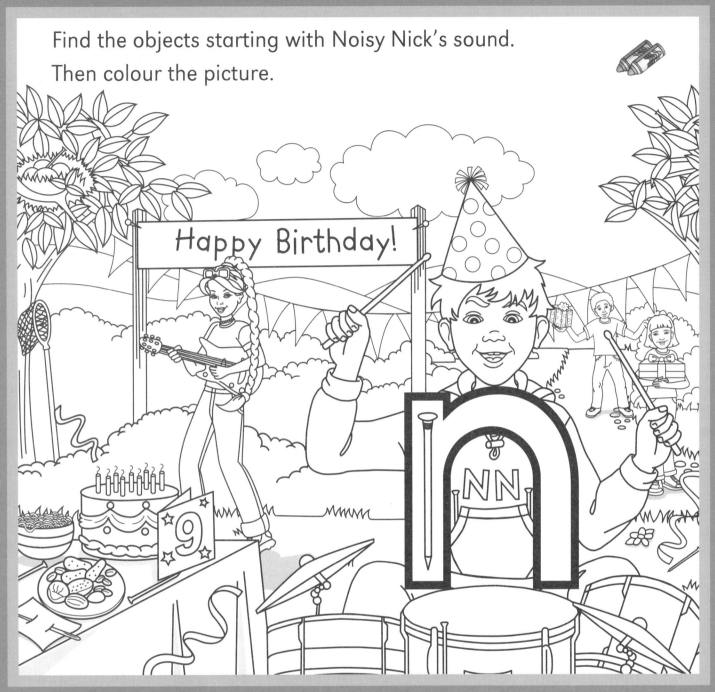

nine   nose   noodles

Focus on sound

Draw lines from Noisy Nick to the things that start with his sound. Circle the one that doesn't.

Draw something that starts with Noisy Nick's sound.

Stick Noisy Nick's letter shape here.

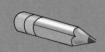

Focus on shape

Let's write Noisy Nick's letter shape.

Let's write both his letter shapes.

Noisy Nick

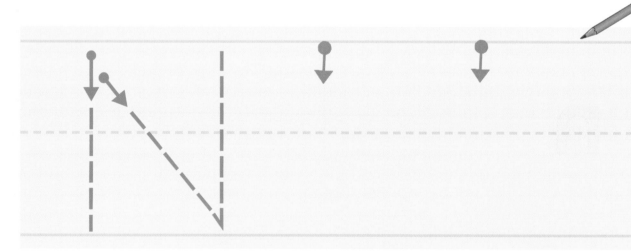

Focus on sound

Find the objects starting with Munching Mike's sound.
Then colour the picture.

map **m**ilk **m**an

Draw lines from Munching Mike to the things that start with his sound. Circle the one that doesn't.

Draw something that starts with Munching Mike's sound.

Stick Munching Mike's letter shape here.

s	k	t	e	i
m	r	c	o	g
a	n	p	u	p

Spell Page 68

c k

a

s

Spell Page 68

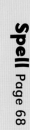

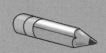

Focus on shape

Let's write Munching Mike's letter shape.

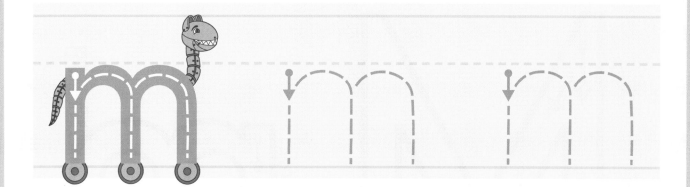

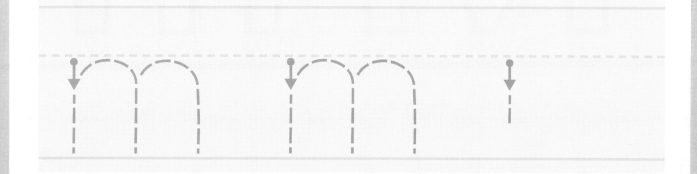

Let's write both his letter shapes.

M m

Munching Mike

Mm Mm Mm

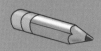

Focus on sound

Find the objects starting with Dippy Duck's sound.
Then colour the picture.

dog   **d**rum   **d**ad

Focus on sound

Draw lines from Dippy Duck to the things that start with her sound. Circle the one that doesn't.

Draw something that starts with Dippy Duck's sound.

Stick Dippy Duck's letter shape here.

Focus on shape

Let's write Dippy Duck's letter shape.

Let's write both her letter shapes.

Dippy Duck

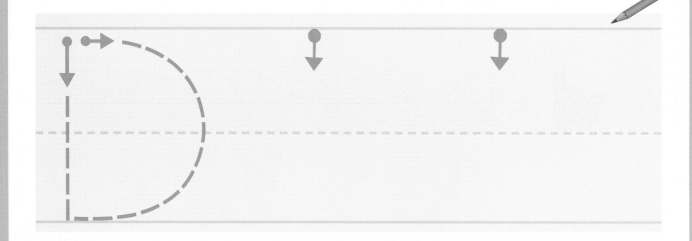

Let's review

Fill in the correct letters to make the words below.

i   n   m   d

_ **ad**

_ **nk**

INDIGO

_ **ine**

9

_ **ap**

Phonic Word Builder

Can you write the two words below? Use the
Letterland characters to help you.

_____ _____ _____

_____ _____ _____

Put the correct Letterland stickers over the plain letter shapes.
Then draw lines to match them to their objects.

i

n

m

d

Letter sound Recognising initial letter sounds is an important first step in language and literacy.

Listen

Listen to the words and put a tick next to the one you hear. The first one has been done for you.

CD 1
Track 35

1.  ✔  ☐  ☐

2. ☐  ☐  ☐

3. ☐  ☐  ☐

4.  ☐  ☐ ☐

5.  ☐  ☐  ☐

6.  ☐ ☐  ☐

Focus on shape

Can you find these characters hidden in the sentences below?
The first words have been done for you.

This is Impy Ink.

Impy thinks of insects.

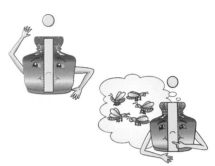

Nick likes the number nine.

Nick reads the newspaper.

Mike likes making music.

Let's meet Mike's Mum.

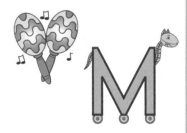

Dippy Duck likes her doll.

Dippy plays the drums.

Focus on sound

Find the objects starting with Golden Girl's sound.
Then colour the picture.

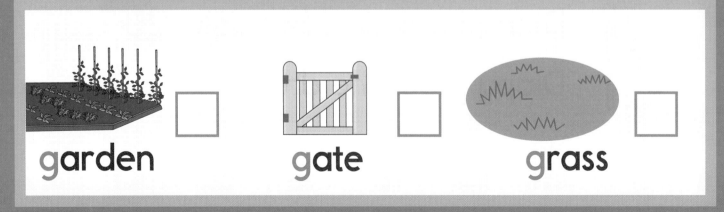

garden   gate   grass

44

Focus on sound

Draw lines from Golden Girl to the things that start with her sound. Circle the one that doesn't.

Draw something that starts with Golden Girl's sound.

Stick Golden Girl's letter shape here.

Let's write Golden Girl's letter shape.

Let's write both her letter shapes.

Golden Girl

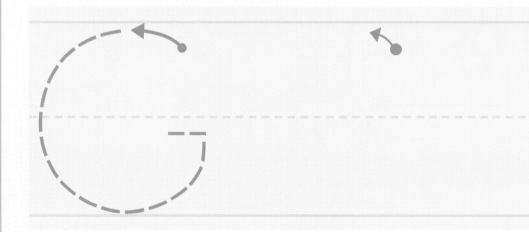

Gg Gg Gg

Focus on sound

Find the objects starting with Oscar Orange's sound.
Then colour the picture.

on   off   orange

Focus on sound

Draw lines from Oscar Orange to the things that start with his sound. Circle the one that doesn't.

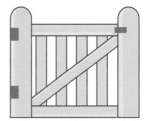

Draw something that starts with Oscar Orange's sound.

Stick Oscar Orange's letter shape here.

Focus on shape

Let's write Oscar Orange's letter shape.

Let's write both his letter shapes.

Oscar Orange

Focus on sound

Find the objects starting with Clever Cat's sound.
Then colour the picture.

cup

car

cake

Focus on sound

Draw lines from Clever Cat to the things that start with her sound. Circle the one that doesn't.

Draw something that starts with Clever Cat's sound.

Stick Clever Cat's letter shape here.

53

Focus on shape

Let's write Clever Cat's letter shape.

Let's write both her letter shapes.

Clever Cat

C c C c C c C c

Focus on sound

Find the objects starting with Kicking King's sound.
Then colour the picture.

key   **k**ettle   **k**itchen

Focus on sound

Draw lines from Kicking King to the things that start with his sound. Circle the one that doesn't.

Kitchen Ideas

Draw something that starts with Kicking King's sound.

Stick Kicking King's letter shape here.

Focus on shape

Let's write Kicking King's letter shape.

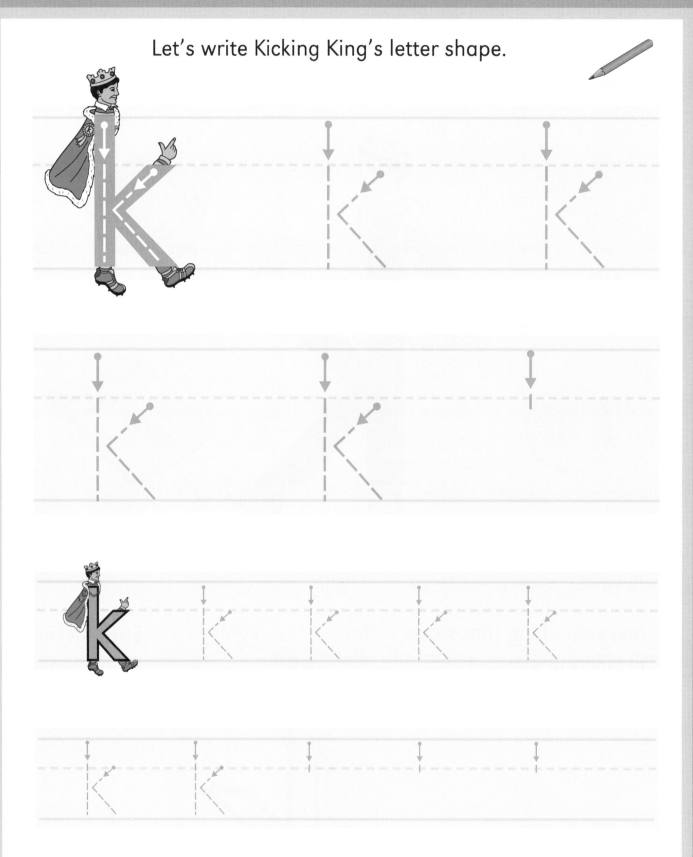

Let's write both his letter shapes.

K k

Kicking King

Kk Kk Kk Kk

Let's review

Fill in the correct letters to make the words below.

g o c k

___ff

___ey

___ate

___up

Phonic Word Builder

Can you write the two words below? Use the
Letterland characters to help you.

_____ _____ _____

_____ _____ _____

61

g

o

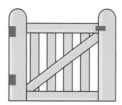

c

k

Letter sound Recognising initial letter sounds is an important first step in language and literacy.

1.  ✓  ☐ ☐

2.  ☐ ☐  ☐

3.  ☐  ☐ ☐

4. ☐ ☐  ☐

5. ☐ ☐ ☐

6.  ☐  ☐ ☐

Focus on shape

Can you find these characters hidden in the sentences below?
The first words have been done for you.

 <u>G</u>olden <u>G</u>irl has a <u>g</u>arden.

Golden Girl grows grapes.

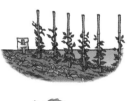

 Oscar is on a dog.

Oscar is on a frog.

 Clever Cat can count.

She can drive a car.

 Kicking King likes kittens.

The king likes kites.

Focus on sound

Find the objects starting with Clever Cat and Kicking King's sound. Then colour the picture.

Clever Cat and **Kicking King** make the same sound. Clever Cat sits behind Kicking King so she isn't kicked.

kick   **sack**   **sock**

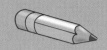

Look at the pictures and say the words. Circle the picture that doesn't end with the '**ck**' sound.

Draw something that ends with a '**ck**' sound.

Let's write Clever Cat's and Kicking King's letter shapes together.

Use your stickers to make these two words.

Letter sound

Say the words out loud. Can you think of any more words with Clever Cat and Kicking King's sound?

Focus on sound

Find the objects starting with Eddy Elephant's sound.
Then colour the picture.

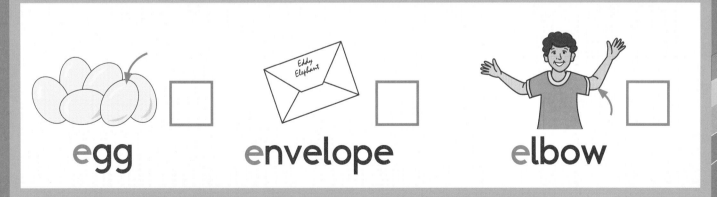

egg   **envelope**   **elbow**

Focus on sound

Draw lines from Eddy Elephant to the things that start with his sound. Circle the one that doesn't.

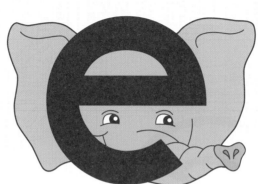

Eddy
Elephant

Draw something that starts with Eddy Elephant's sound.

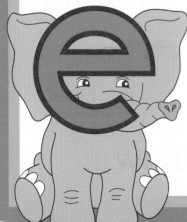

Stick Eddy Elephant's letter shape here.

Let's write Eddy Elephant's letter shape.

Let's write both his letter shapes.

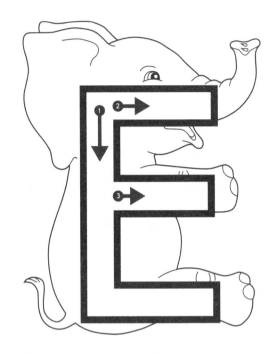

Eddy Elephant

Focus on sound

Find the objects starting with Uppy Umbrella's sound.
Then colour the picture.

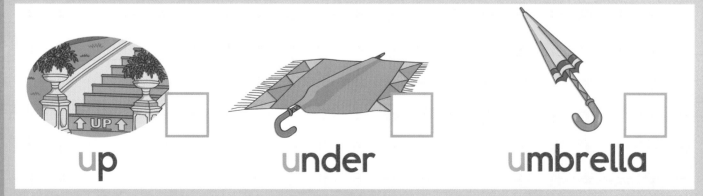

up   under   umbrella

Focus on sound

Draw lines from Uppy Umbrella to the things that start with her sound. Circle the one that doesn't.

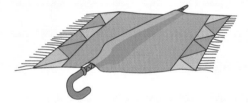

Draw something that starts with Uppy Umbrella's sound.

Stick Uppy Umbrella's letter shape here.

Focus on shape

Let's write Uppy Umbrella's letter shape.

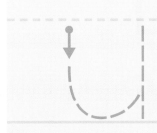

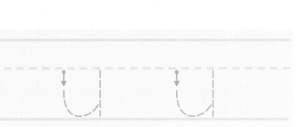

Let's write both her letter shapes.

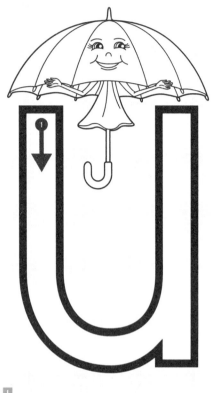

Uppy Umbrella

Uu Uu Uu Uu

Focus on sound

Find the objects starting with Red Robot's sound.
Then colour the picture.

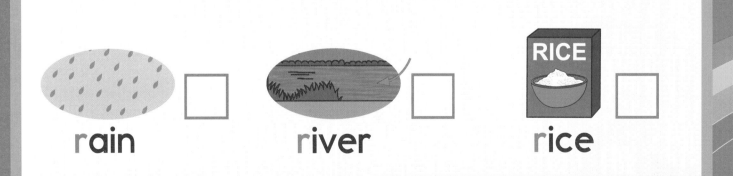

rain river rice

Focus on sound

Draw lines from Red Robot to the things that start with his sound. Circle the one that doesn't.

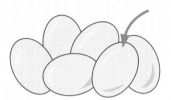

RICE

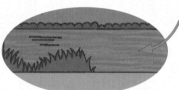

Draw something that starts with Red Robot's sound.

Stick Red Robot's letter shape here.

Focus on shape

Let's write Red Robot's letter shape.

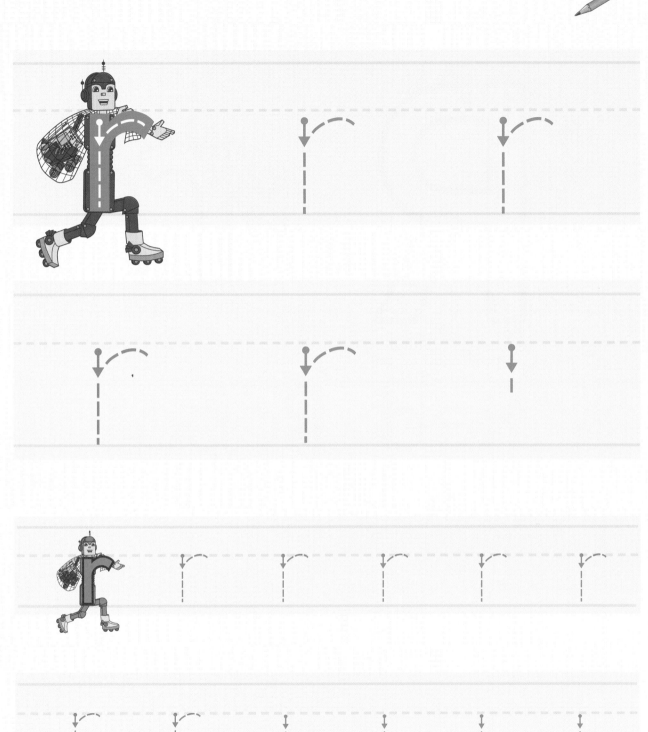

Let's write both his letter shapes.

Red Robot

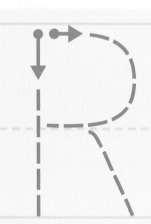

Rr Rr Rr Rr

Let's review

Fill in the correct letters to make the words below.

c k e u r

_ p

s a _ _

_ e d

_ g g

81

Phonic Word Builder

Draw lines to match the words to the pictures.

duck

sun

pen

10

ten

red

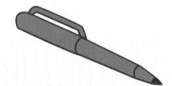

Now can you write this whole word?

Review Put the correct Letterland stickers over the plain letter shapes.
Then draw lines to match them to their objects.

e

RICE

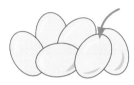

u

r

Letter sound Recognising initial letter sounds is an important first step in language and literacy.

83

Listen

Listen to the words and put a tick next to the one you hear. The first one has been done for you.

CD 1

Track 68

1.  RICE ☐    ✓    ☐

2.  ☐    ☐    ☐

3.  ☐    ☐    ☐

4.   ☐    ☐    RICE ☐

5.  ☐    ☐   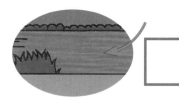 ☐

6.  ☐   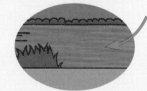 ☐    ☐

Focus on shape

Can you find these characters hidden in the sentences below?
The first words have been done for you.

<u>E</u>ddy is in b<u>e</u>d.

He has seven egg cups.

Uppy is under a bug.

Uppy is upside down.

Red Robot can run.

He can ride a raft!

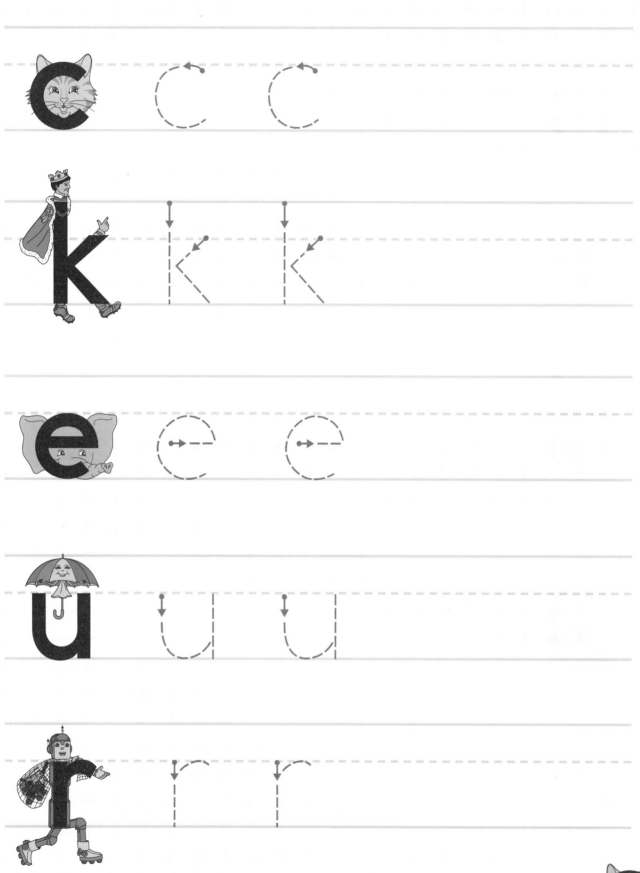

c c c

k k k

e e e

u u u

r r r

Congratulations! You're ready for Student Book 2.